CRUMLIN to PONTYMISTER
Over the Years

by
Brian Collins

This book is dedicated to my wife, Barbara,
for putting up with me 'over the years'.

Foreword by
Dr. John Herbert M.A., O.B.E.

*Any profits accrued by the author through the
publication and sale of this book will be donated to*
Ty Hafan, The Children's Hospice in Wales.
*The hospice, under the patronage of
H.R.H. The Prince of Wales,
aims to improve the quality of life of children
with life-limiting or life-threatening conditions,
by providing a high standard of respite
and palliative care, engendered in a caring,
therapeutic and family atmosphere.*

Old Bakehouse Publications

Abertillery

First published in October 2007

ISBN 978-1-905967-06-3

Published in the U.K. by
Old Bakehouse Publications
Church Street,
Abertillery, Gwent NP13 1EA
Telephone: 01495 212600 Fax: 01495 216222
e-mail: theoldbakeprint@btconnect.com
www.oldbakehouseprint.co.uk

Made and printed in the UK
by J.R. Davies (Printers) Ltd.

British Library Cataloguing in Publication Data: a catalogue
record for this book is available from the British Library.

Foreword

When well over a half-century ago I came down the Sirhowy valley for the first time and later became familiar with the Ebbw valley, the buses passed coal tips, pits, run-down communities of terraced houses, narrow roads, derelict buildings, tiny corner shops. Here was the evidence of a district where grew up a warm and generous people, but severely underprivileged, exploited, poverty- stricken and enduring constant hardship. The harsh and dangerous conditions of working hundreds of yards below the ground in the pits to hew out coal are no more. Every ton of coal that came down the valleys had blood on it. The explosions underground sent to an early grave hundreds of men and boys barely past their twelfth birthday, leaving grief-stricken wives and mothers, destitute and abandoned. Nowadays if we care to look around, to travel from Pontymister northwards to Crumlin has become a spiritual and aesthetic experience. The scars of the industrial despoilment of our ancient mountains and valleys have now been removed; forests cover the hillsides, new roads are bordered by flower beds and trees, the streets lead to renewed communities. The matchless beauty of our environment catches the breath for those with eyes to see.

But we must not forget those bygone days that gave us birth and formed us. We are still a warm and generous people. This book serves to remind us of that past, its former glory in our churches, chapels and schools, its vibrant communities and the ultimate achievements of our people in education, health and moderate prosperity against the odds.

Here presented for us is the record of our history from those dark days to the present. Throughout its pages the hope of the human spirit, never dimmed by adversity, has now emerged in triumph. Education was brought to the valley by good schools and excellent teachers. Former pupils have reached the commanding heights of all professions. Members of Parliament and the Assembly of Wales have been dispatched to Westminster and Cardiff to serve the interests of ordinary people who now no longer bow the knee or touch their caps to their 'betters'.

Here presented for us is the record of a community that need not be ashamed of its past, but can be proud of its present. Here is a record in which I have been involved and I commend this book to all my fellow citizens who want either to recall the days of past years or, still young, want to find and study their roots. I am privileged to write my good will into the record.

John Herbert,

Dr. John Herbert M.A., O.B.E.
Headmaster of Pontywaun and Newbridge Grammar Schools, 1959-1975.

Contents

Introduction

It is some twenty-five years since the first Crumlin to Pontymister book was produced, in co-authorship with Terry Powell. Much has changed since that time. The A467 bypass road has for instance had a dramatic effect on some of the villages along its route. The removal of heavy and dangerous traffic has been very beneficial, but the detour of through traffic has meant that many businesses along the old main roads have lost out. Some residential properties have unfortunately been affected by the bypass, both as an obstruction and as a source of noise.

The heavy industries of coal mining and steel-making have given way to many light industrial undertakings. The resulting improvement in the atmosphere is clear to see, with substantial growth of greenery in recent years. The water courses of the River Ebbw and the canal (such as it now is) are far less polluted, although further improvement is still needed.

The earlier books concentrated on the past, with their publisher requiring photographs to be at least forty years old. Now, with a more open attitude towards the contents of this book, the title itself indicates that the intention is to look at the history of the valley's people, from early beginnings right up to the present time.

This stretch of the 'Western Valley' has seen a wealth of skills and abilities - academic, professional, technical and sporting to name just a few. Entertainers and sports persons have performed not just locally but internationally. Within these pages an attempt has been made to trace the history of some of these successes, with written accounts invited from persons having close knowledge of them, giving valuable authenticity.

This type of project provides an opportunity to meet up with persons not encountered for very many years - very fulfilling experiences. The title of the book, 'Over the Years', suggests an attempt to look into this period, perhaps wondering where we have been and what we have been doing all this time.

Changes in administration have been experienced, moving from the Abercarn and Risca Urban District Councils to Islwyn Borough Council, and more recently to Caerphilly County Borough Council. Nationally, devolution has seen the setting up of the Welsh Assembly.

A new facility which can be used to view and to admire old photographs is the Internet. Several excellent local web sites are available. Some of these are mentioned under Acknowledgements. In addition, most sports clubs have websites, and those that haven't are often to be found under some other guise through an Internet search.

The author has found the operators of these web sites to be very helpful in the preparation of this book, with due acknowledgement made. Needless to say, also, that all the persons approached in the search for photographs and information have been extremely helpful. This has made the work much easier and more enjoyable. Sales of this book will again benefit *Ty Hafan, The Children's Hospice in Wales*, making the project that much more worthwhile.

Brian Colens

Brian Collins

1. Crumlin Viaduct.

Chapter 1

Around the Towns

2. Main Street, Crumlin in the 1950s. No great traffic problems even along the main thoroughfare. The Viaduct Tavern on the right has now become the WEXA Club, and the whole area has been transformed by the building of the bypass road.

3. Crumlin Square at about the same time, looking back along Main Street to the left, with Hillside to the right. The block directly ahead, which contained the Empress Cinema, has been completely removed and replaced by the Old Age Pensioners' Centre. The Workmen's Institute on the extreme right still stands, and is utilized by Caerphilly County Borough Council for educational purposes.

4. A 1930s view over the river bridge at Crumlin towards Hafodyrynys Hill. The bus ahead was turning towards Llanhilleth. Bethel Baptist chapel is seen beyond the bus.

5. The same scene in 2007. The old bridge is now closed to traffic as is the immediate access to Hafodyrynys Hill. The old road, which the bus in the above picture was taking, is now closed to traffic owing to instability. The bus route to Llanhilleth follows a roundabout route up the hill and back through Soffrydd. The A467 bypass road is seen in the foreground.

6. The subway at Newbridge in the 1930s. The roads were relatively free of vehicles, but there soon became a need to install traffic lights. The Jones's bus was cautiously turning towards Crumlin.

7. Traffic lights now control the greater number of vehicles passing through. Larger vehicles also require a measure of the bridge height to be displayed. Attempts to make the scene more attractive have been made by way of a mural on the bridge and a model village on the bank ahead. Danger to pedestrians walking under the subway has led to a proposal to construct a footbridge, from the lower end of High Street, over the railway and the river, to lead towards the Comprehensive School and the Leisure Centre.

8. Looking over the lower part of Newbridge from the park, before the development of the Pant estate. Zoah Chapel is seen at the bottom of the slope, together with the Grand Cinema on the extreme left. Celynen South Colliery was tipping its waste in the base of the valley at that time.

9. Abercarn and Chapel of Ease in the early 1900s - the house standing alone on Pantyresk Road was built in 1901. Abercarn House can be seen amongst the trees in the centre, and lower down, the tin Church of St. Luke's, opened in 1890. Other places of worship in the picture are Cae'r Gorlan in West End, (opened in 1883), and Garn on High Street, which was built in 1847.

10. Chapel of Ease photographed from West End before the development of the Persondy estate, the main feature being the outdoor swimming baths in the centre.

11. The same view in April 2007 shows the cleared site where the swimming baths once stood. Part of it is taken up by the car park for the school to the left. Behind the school are houses and bungalows built on the ground where Abercarn House was located. Houses of the Persondy estate can be seen amongst the trees to the right. The walkway to West End has been disturbed by the current housing development spilling over from the old Celynen South Colliery site.

12./13. Benjamin Hall II was married to Charlotte, the daughter of Richard Crawshay from whom the couple inherited the ironworks and the coal mines at Abercarn. This led to their living at Abercarn House, shown above. He was responsible for the construction of Hall's tramroad, which dramatically improved the transportation of coal to the docks at Newport. His son, Benjamin Hall III, was to become Lord Llanofer, marrying Augusta Waddington, the heiress of Llanofer, in 1823. Benjamin was elected to Parliament in 1831 as member for Monmouth Boroughs. As First Commissioner for Works, he oversaw the construction of the bell to be installed in the clock tower at Westminster. The bell, to this day, has the nickname 'Big Ben'.

The nearest church to Abercarn House was the parish church at Mynyddislwyn. For this reason a small chapel of ease was built at nearby Celynen - now called Chapel of Ease. This enabled family and employees of the Halls to attend Church without having to encounter the arduous journey to the top of Mynyddislwyn mountain.

In 1853 Lord and Lady Llanofer erected the Welsh Church at Abercarn for worship in the Welsh language, with the Service of the Established Anglican

Church. A changing population led to difficulties in continuing the Church in this way, leading to conversion to a Welsh Presbyterian Church. Services are still held periodically in Welsh, but the building is predominantly used by St. Luke's Church, whose own building has had to be vacated. In 1859, Benjamin Hall III became Baron Llanofer of Llanofer and Abercarn. He died in 1867.

Lady Llanofer was a staunch teetotaller, who bought all the public houses in the district and converted them into tea houses - typically The Cloch at Abercarn (see page 34). She sponsored many things Welsh, and actually published books of recipes and on Welsh costume.

Lady Llanofer outlived her husband by more than twenty-eight years, dying in 1896 at the age of 94.

14. Abercarn Urban District included the villages of Crumlin, Trinant, Hafodyrynys, Newbridge, Pentwynmawr, Abercarn and Cwmcarn. Formed in 1894, its official seal showed the Westminster clock tower in recognition of Benjamin Hall, after whom the clock's bell was nicknamed, (see page 12). The Council Offices were built on the site of an intensely used Market Hall, which was built in 1846. The District Council was absorbed into Islwyn Borough Council in 1974. The Council Offices were demolished in 1979 and the residential complex of Gwyddon Court erected in their place.

15.

16. Edward VII succeeded to the throne upon the death of Queen Victoria in 1901. The Coronation date was set for 26th June 1902, but, due to illness, it was postponed until 9th August 1902. Just hope the ticket was still valid!

17. Looking along Islwyn Street in Abercarn's West End, c1955. Straight ahead is Troedyrhiw, and higher on the hillside, Pantyresk Road.

18. The same view in April 2007. Of the many shops in the first picture, only the West End Post Office remains. Several have been converted into dwelling houses, whilst the large block on the right-hand side, which contained two shops, has been totally removed. The result is a clearer view of 'Eynon's Corner', where the road turns through ninety degrees towards Newbridge. Many more vehicles now use the road, hence the traffic-calming humps.

19. A sombre morning image of the demolition of The Ranks on High Street, Abercarn, in 1983. The Ranks, dating back to the late 1840s, were originally made up of four rows. They were built by Ebenezer Rogers and were once described as a 'Model Village'.

20. The site is now occupied by blocks of flats, the complex still bearing the name of The Ranks.

21. An image to remember for all those who worked at the National Coal Board's No. 6 Area Headquarters at Abercarn. The building is now used for private commercial purposes, and the canal has been overlain by the bypass road.

22. In March 2007, we see that the building of the bypass road and the vigorous growth of trees in the area have all but obliterated the view of the old offices, now used for industrial purposes. The chapel on the left, first built by the Methodist Church, is still used as a Full Gospel Mission.

23. Looking towards Abercarn from the Spiteful, c1910. Few houses on Rhyswg Road had been built at that time. The English Baptist Chapel is seen in the centre, and Chapel Farm on the extreme right. The welfare ground was later to be developed from the farm's fields to the left.

24. Chapel Farm, Cwmcarn, showing the houses of Beech Terrace at the Spiteful, on the lower slopes of Mynyddislwyn Mountain. The farm was built on the site of an earlier monastery, the graveyard of which was discovered when the foundations for nearby Chapel Farm Terrace were being dug - hence the nickname for the terrace as 'Skeleton Row'. The farm lands are now occupied by Cwmcarn High School, (previously Cwmcarn Comprehensive School).

25. Crowd at the opening of Cwmcarn New Park in 1913.

26. A view of the Park, with the rear of Chapel Farm Terrace ahead, and the houses of The Spiteful on the hillside in the distance. On the extreme right are the ramshackle structures along what was locally known as 'Pig's Lane'. The Park was later to be dug up for allotments, and later still to be developed for light industry - initially the Crescent Toys factory, but currently the site is occupied by Solectron Wales.

27. An old view looking north along Newport Road, Cwmcarn. The white cottage on the right was replaced in 1913 by Park Hall Cinema.

28. The same view some years later, by which time Park Hall had been built, together with Cwmcarn Library & Institute, seen on the left. On the immediate left are the Co-operative Stores, and a little further along Jack Hatfield's Bicycle shop.

29. The flags are out at Jamesville, Cwmcarn, to celebrate the Coronation in 1953. The road had not been surfaced at that time, so a big clean up was underway - possibly in preparation for a street party.

30. Factory Trip, Cwmcarn, 1925, showing Twyncarn House standing proud above the lock-keeper's cottage and Staite's Billiards Hall. The name of the hill came from being the main access from Cwmcarn to the Flannel Factory at its lower end. In 1875, a dam holding back the water in a feeder reservoir burst. This caused the factory to be flooded and its owner John Hunt, his wife, and four children died, together with two of his servants and an apprentice.

31. The canal at Pontywaun in the 1930s. The view of the Castle Inn is now blocked by properties built on the strip of land between the waterway and the road.

32. A property at Crosskeys, known as The Pandy, on the site where Pandy Park was later developed.

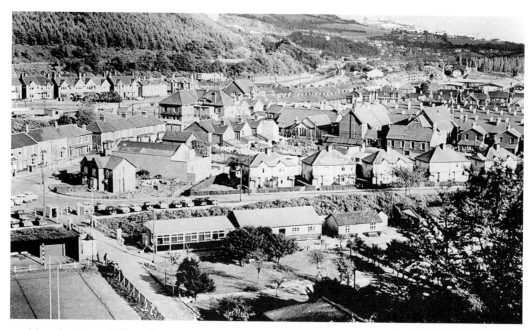

33. A view of Crosskeys taken from the hillside above Pandy Park in the mid 1960s. Many of the buildings seen, such as the Miners' Institute and the Primitive Methodist Church, have disappeared. The river has been diverted to make way for the A467 bypass road, resulting in a new entrance to the Park off Gladstone Street, and the relocation of Crosskeys R.F.C.'s Clubhouse.

34. The Round House, Crosskeys, which was originally built as a toll house by the Abercarn Turnpike Trust Commissioners. In its modern renovated form, it has been used as a dwelling house for many years. Past residents have included the well known Welsh rugby team trainer Ray Lewis, who was later followed in the post by his son Gerry.

35. Houses in Tir-y-Cwm Road, once commanding a clear view of Risca. The photograph was taken over the bridge on Dan-y-Graig Road. The same view is now completely obliterated by the bypass road.

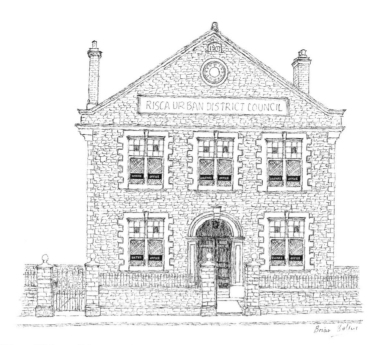

36. Risca Urban District Council was formed in 1878 of Risca parish and those parts of Upper and Lower Machen from the Ebbw river to the top of Mynydd Machen, to include Ochyrwyth, the copperworks area (Danygraig and the Sugar Loaf), the Risca Blackvein Colliery and its houses, the Full Moon area, and a little later, that part of Mynyddyslwyn parish where the new pit and Newtown were built. Risca UDC eventually became part of Islwyn Borough Council, and in more recent local government re-organisation joined Islwyn and Rhymney Valley Borough Councils to form Caerphilly County Borough Council. The building is now used as rehearsal rooms by the Risca Male Choir (see page 125).

37. The opening of Risca Urban District Council Offices in 1907.

38. A view of Risca taken from Dan-y-Graig towards the steelworks. Although vital to the early development of the valley towns, the heavy industries brought along a heavy burden in the pollution which they created. The cleaner air since their demise has certainly triggered vigorous growth in vegetation. The bypass road now rather changes this view.

39. The Palace Cinema, Risca, seen in its better days in the 1950s.

40. The Palace being renovated in 2007, having stood in a derelict state for many years. Plans are afoot to develop the building so as to contain a library and a store, together with Local Authority offices.

Chapter 2

Trade, Industry & Transport

41. T. W. Kennard, designer of Crumlin Viaduct, standing proud on its soon to be completed surface. A great deal has been written on the history of the viaduct, and for much of this the reader is referred to to the excellent website www.crumlinviaduct.co.uk. Work on the first of the piers began in 1853, and the structure was finished in 1857. Its length was 1,650 feet, and its maximum height 200 feet. It was claimed to be the longest railway viaduct in the world at the time, and remained as the longest Warren girder form of structure for many more years. (A Warren girder is a triangulated truss made up of a series of sloping members set between horizontal top and bottom members. It has no vertical elements. This configuration was devised by James Warren).

42. An early view of the canal with the viaduct as a backdrop, and the lock-keeper trudging his way along the towpath. The canal terminated at Crumlin with a turning pool.

43. An engraving published in The Illustrated London News, December 1854, depicting Crumlin Viaduct under construction. The equidistant piers were built 150 feet apart.

44. Another engraving depicting the opening of the viaduct on June 1st 1857. Twenty thousand people were reported to have attended, with volleys of cannon fire throughout the day. The designer, T. W. Kennard, later entertained some two hundred guests to dinner at his residence, Crumlin Hall.

45. An artist's impression of Crumlin Low Level Station, with the viaduct as a backdrop, providing a very smokey scene.

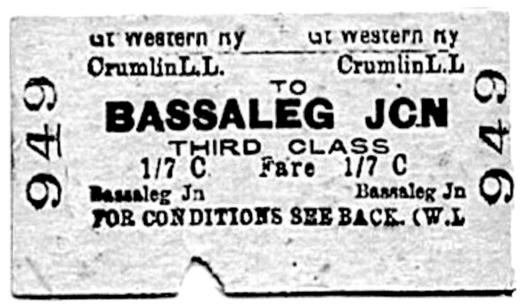

46. Difficult to imagine nowadays travelling from Crumlin to Bassaleg for 1 shilling and 7 pence, (about 8p)!

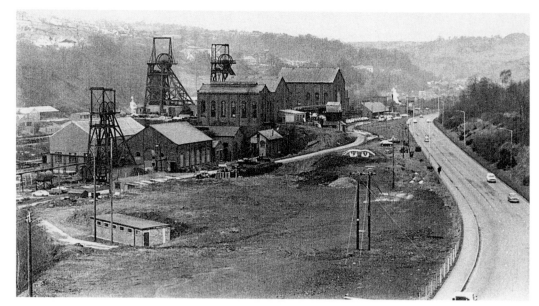

47. An unusual view of Celynen North Colliery, Newbridge, taken from an elevated position above the bypass, the latter following the line of the old canal. The smaller headgear to the left belongs to the Graig Fawr pit. Coal was first produced in 1916 by the Newport Abercarn Blackvein Coal Company. During the last few years of its life it was linked underground to Oakdale colliery where its coal was raised to the surface and, with Oakdale, it closed in 1989.

48. Canal lock at Newbridge. The stacks of Celynen South Colliery can be seen ahead, with its imposing refuse tip almost filling the base of the valley - its later removal made way for playing fields. The colliery site itself is currently being developed, with a large estate of mixed dwellings under construction.

49. A familiar image for so many miners at Celynen South Colliery as they approached the pithead baths from the canteen. The headgear of No. 1 Pit is seen in the centre and the aerial ropeway, carrying waste to the mountain-top tip, to the left. The photograph was taken just days after the colliery ceased production in 1985.

50. The scene in February 2007 with the colliery long gone. Development of the cleared site is well under way through the construction of an estate of mixed dwellings.

51. The canal bridge at Chapel of Ease in more picturesque times. At this point the canal has been replaced by the A467 bypass.

52. Mr. John Franchi, proprietor of John's Café in Abercarn, photographed a few days before it was closed in September 1970. The café was opened in 1949 by a man who had received a commendation for bravery from Field Marshall Alexander. Mr. Franchi was born in South Wales but was forced to spend the war years in Italy, where he worked with the partisans helping allied servicemen to escape or to evade capture. The Victoria Hall complex, of which John's Café formed a part, was soon afterwards demolished to make way for the new bypass road.

53. The original Knight Bros, Abercarn, came about in 1935, when Harold (Chum) Knight (pictured left), and his brother Joe began a decorating business. Some years later, Chum's son Paul left school at the age of 15 and joined his father in the trade. Six years later still, another son, Keith, took his place in the family's business by working at the company's DIY shop in High Street. This was one of the oldest buildings in Abercarn, a section of it once being a malt house. It was also thought to have been be an old ironworks company store. Upon Chum's death in 1973, the decorating part of the business was closed, and Paul joined his brother to concentrate on the retail and trade outlets. Another shop was opened in Bridge Street, to be managed by Paul and his wife Irene, whilst Keith, along with his wife, Christine, continued plying their trade at High Street, ably assisted by Chum's widow, Iris, and staff.

54. The Knight brothers and wives, Keith, Christine, Irene and Paul, opposite the High Street shop.

55. The High Street shop was closed in 2001, and the building converted into flats. The block is now named The Malthouse. The business continued at the Bridge Street premises for a short period before being sold - (the closing down sale is pictured left). 'Knight Bros' still exists at a different location in Bridge Street, but under new ownership.

(Ref: Paul and Keith Knight)

33

56. The Cloch Gobaith Temperance Hotel, Abercarn. Its location was at the bottom of Twyn Road - the Welsh Church can be seen amongst the trees.

57. The bridge over the canal at Abercarn provided access to Prince of Wales Colliery. The building on the left was the lamproom, used as a temporary mortuary at the time of the great explosion. It is still standing and is used for commercial purposes.

58./59. Two unusual views of Prince of Wales Colliery, Abercarn. The upper picture is taken across the main road and the canal. The large refuse tip in the background to the left was only removed with the development of the Prince of Wales Industrial Estate in 1969. The small buildings to the lower left became the engineering drawing and surveying offices under the National Coal Board. The lower picture was taken from the yard next to the workshops, c1910. The colliery will forever remain famous for the explosion in 1878, when 264 lives were lost.

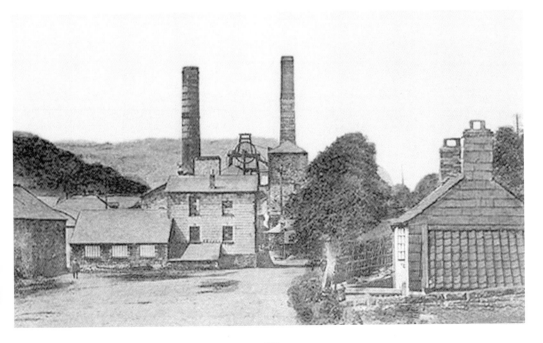

60 The Black Bridge on the Well Road which linked Commercial Road/Newport Road to Chapel Farm.

61. The author seen taking a liking to Carini's ice cream at Marne Street, Cwmcarn, in 1935. Carini's shop on Newport Road was vacated in the 1940s. The premises were then used by the British Restaurant, and few will have forgotten the meals served there!

62. Proudly displaying his Penny-Farthing bicycle is Bill Partridge, from Cwmcarn, for many years President of Cwmcarn Paragon Cycling Club. The cycle is now housed in the Risca Industrial Museum.

The Penny-Farthing is also referred to as the 'High' or 'Ordinary' bicycle, and the first one was invented in 1871 by British engineer, James Starley. The Penny Farthing came after the development of the 'Hobbyhorse', and the French 'Velocipede' or 'Boneshaker', all versions of early bikes. However, the Penny Farthing was the first really efficient bicycle, consisting of a small rear wheel and large front wheel pivoting on a simple tubular frame with tyres of rubber.

63. An early image of the Castle Inn at Pontywaun. It seems to have originated from two separate properties - a house and a shop, perhaps the block earlier still simply comprised two houses.

64. These beginnings might not easily be identified from the building's present facade, but the only major construction has been to eliminate the right-hand door.

65. This advertisement for Dunn's Garage appeared in 1916. The business was established by Elias Henry Dunn in Gladstone Street, Crosskeys, c1910, selling hand-pumped Pratt's petrol. It was later moved to Risca Road following the need for larger premises. Elias opened another outlet in the now closed 'Nutmegs' shop in Risca, when he also began, along with Russell Cuff (of Cuff's Billiards Hall, Crosskeys), the first passenger bus service in the area.

66. The picture below, taken in 1935, shows Elias Dunn's son Wilf on the right.

67. Dunn's Garage on Risca Road, Crosskeys, photographed in the mid 1950s. An expansion saw the British Legion Hall, appearing to the right of the picture, being taken over as a showroom. Brothers Wilf and Alf kept the garage going until the early 1970s. Mr. Dunn Senior took an active part in the business side of things, and could be seen riding his old black Rudge bicycle between his home in Gladstone Street and the garage until he was well into his eighties. A garage business has since continued on the same site, but under new ownership.

(Sam Lewis)

68. Old Blackvein Colliery, Crosskeys, opened in 1845 by the Risca Iron and Coal Company. It suffered several serious explosions, and was finally closed in 1921. Risca Colliery can be seen in the background.

69. Waunfawr Brickworks, Risca, built in 1844, was originally owned by John Russell, and subsequently, by 1910, by the Star Brick and Tile Company, ceasing production in 1918.

70. A striking view of the disintegrating Long Bridge at Risca, at the point at which it diverted from the Sirhowy Line, photographed in 1900. The bridge was built around 1810 to carry the Sirhowy Tramroad over the valley. It had thirty three arches in its construction, and was demolished soon after this photograph was taken.

71. The last train out of Risca Station in 1962, prior to the discontinuation of the valley's passenger service. At the time of writing, the line is being renovated in preparation for the reopening of a service from Ebbw Vale to Cardiff. Stations are being established at Newbridge, Crosskeys and Risca.

72. William Morgan Baulch, seen here leading a funeral along Tredegar Street in Risca in the late 1920s, served in the army during the First World War, and soon afterwards joined his uncle's undertaker's business in Newport. He later set up himself in Maryland Road, Pontymister (near the Britannia Inn), later moving to Commercial Street. He died in 1966, never having retired. The business was continued by his sons Ron and Arthur until it was sold in 1979, following the disastrous floods in the district.

73. Motorised vehicles had taken over from the horse-drawn variety when the impressive photograph above was taken. The decorations on the building indicate a celebration year in the mid to late 1930s.

74. Tom Chivers of Risca with his bus fully laden for a trip in the late 1930s. Second from the left standing is Mr. Chivers' wife Gwendoline.

75. Risca Lending Library and Music Store as it looked around the 1930s. The film showing at the Palace Cinema sums up the dilapidated condition of the building in 2007. Plans are afoot to redevelop it, with a library being one of its new sections.

76./77. The Pontymister ironworks began in 1801. First it was connected by a tramroad to the canal, but when the tramroad from Newport to Sirhowy was opened in 1805, the ironworks tramroad was connected to the Sirhowy tramroad. In the 1830s much pig iron was received from the Cwm Celyn and Blaina ironworks near the head of the valley, and bar iron sent to Newport.

All of the various owners of the Pontymister ironworks for the first forty years were in financial difficulties, and most were bankrupted. The sale notice from an 1806 newspaper following the first such bankruptcy reveals that there were 19 workmen's houses within the works site.

Eventually, the works was purchased by the Banks brothers around 1845 and became a tinplate works. They prospered, and Pontymister as we know it today began to grow. Beerhouses, public houses, commercial hotels, shops and houses grew up around the entrance to the works (note some of the names - the Rolling Mill, the Forge Hammer). More development took place along the main road to the north. The Monmouthshire Canal Company's tramroad was converted into a railway in 1850 and the Britannia Foundry, opened by Charles Jordan in 1854 alongside the railway line.

P. S. Phillips, owner of the Abertillery tinplate works, purchased the Pontymister tinplate works in 1880, trading as the Pontymister Tin Plate Company. He added a steelworks, erected at a cost of £30,000, to make 1,000 tons of steel per week by the Siemens process to supply Pontymister and his other works. His wife was the daughter of Edward Robothan of Risca, a surgeon, whose house, The Grove, is the present Oxford House. They lived at Crumlin Hall. In June 1891 Congressman William McKinley, later the 25th President of the United States, brought about the imposition of a tariff on imported tinplate to enable the USA to build up its own tinplate industry. This led to a demand for tinplate at a lower price to compensate for the tariff. All works produced to full capacity,

new mills being erected everywhere, producing a glut of tinplate. By 1893, the Pontymister tinplate works comprised 12 mills.

The company was bankrupt in 1896 and eventually purchased by Henry White and Company, who owned the Pontymister foundry. In 1921 this company amalgamated with Messrs Partridge, Jones and John Paton, Limited. The last ingot was rolled on 20th January 1962, some mill employees, also in the local Territorial Army unit, bringing their bugles to sound the last post. The works completely closed with the opening of Llanwern steelworks.

With the closing of Broad's foundry in 2004, so ended 200 years of iron-making in Risca.

(Tony Jukes)

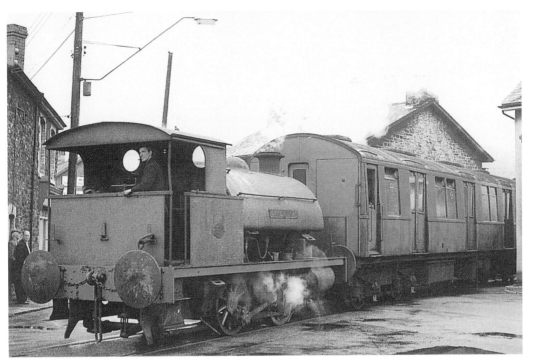

78. Most of the London Transport F stock built in 1920 was scrapped at Pontymister Steelworks by Birds of Risca between 1963 and 1964. The photograph shows the trailing end of DM car 4635 being towed over the crossing in June 1963.

79. Employees of Suflex Ltd. at Pontymister, about to set off on their annual trip laid on by the company, c1961.

Chapter 3

Education

80. Crumlin High Level School, opened in 1912, set against a backdrop of the viaduct.

81. Staff at Crumlin High Level School in the mid 1930s. Back Row, left to right:- ? ?, Mr. Hughes, Miss Chambers, Mr. Cule, Miss Hughes. Front Row:- Miss Hume, Mr. Barnes, Mr. Max Thomas, (Headmaster), Miss Jones and Mr. Jones.

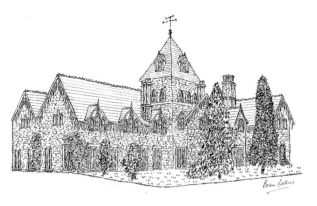

82./83. During the late nineteenth century and the early twentieth century coal mining became the main development in South East Wales, employing tens of thousands of miners. Such was the pace of technological developments in mining, coupled with the many accidents and major disasters (nationally as well as in South Wales), that in 1911 Parliament brought in the Coal Mines Act.

This Act broadly required a high degree of competency in those managing and supervising mining operations. Inevitably this led to the requirement of an organised system of education and training. The Coal Owners Association of the day needed to set up a centre capable of achieving this objective, and Crumlin Hall proved to be the best available, both in terms of size and geographical location.

Crumlin Hall was built in 1853 by T. W. Kennard and was the base for his supervision of the building of the Crumlin Viaduct, itself a major feat of engineering and a well-known landmark for over 100 years.

The Crumlin College, (better known locally as the Mining School) as initially set up was opened in 1914 with James Dobbie, a Scot, as Principal. He retained this position until just after the end of the Second World War. For the first fifteen years or so, the subjects studied were all mining disciplines focused on ensuring a high standard of scientific application to mining engineering, both for production techniques and safety considerations.

At the end of this first period the college came under the control of the Local Education Authority. This authority recognised the many changes that were taking place in local industry at this time and understood the need for a wider spectrum of studies to be available in the area in addition to the traditional mining themes. Consequently the college became The Monmouthshire Mining and Technical College.

This expansion of studies saw new courses in mechanical and electrical engineering, chemistry, and commercial studies. Following the Second World War Dr T. V. Starkey became the college Principal, and it was at this time that the courses offered expanded greatly. During this expansion of studies following World War Two (in 1948 in fact) the title was again changed to reflect the wider pull of students, thus becoming The Technical College Monmouthshire.

In order to accommodate the expansion of student numbers, extra classrooms, laboratories and workshop facilities were provided by the construction of prefabricated outbuildings whilst the safe and continued use of Crumlin Hall itself was facilitated by the addition of external steel buttresses in order to mitigate subsidence damage.

This continual increase in student numbers meant that by the late 1950s it was obvious that a new site would be required for the college, and this was to be at Crosskeys. This then became the main site for the college in 1961. Crumlin Hall continued in use for a few years after this before finally being demolished in 1967.

(Clive Jones)

84. Staff at Tynewydd Junior and Infants School, c1989. Back Row, left to right:-
Sam Lewis, Mrs. Janet Caddick, Mrs. Marion Case (Secretary), Mrs. Guinevere
James, Mrs. Sandra Ward, and Mrs. Sylvia Amin (Nursery Nurse). Front Row, left
to right:- Mrs. Joan Powell, Deputy Head Mrs. Barbara Collins, Headmaster
Malcolm Ford, Mrs. Joyce Mayers and Mrs. Kath Godwin.

85. Nativity Play at Tynewydd Infants School, Newbridge, in 1968, with
Elizabeth Collins as Mary, and Alun Thoms as Joseph. Others in the picture, from
left to right:- Niel Pfeiffer, Neil Davies, Keith Herbert and Christopher Hopkins.

86. Mrs. J. Davies with her class at Tynewydd Infants School, 1974, with Head Mrs. Thomas on the right. Back Row, left to right:- Simon Collins, Stephen Haines, Gavin Thomas, Stephen Shafer, Paul Deverill, ?.?, Simon Powell, Shaun Davies and Mark Beard. Second Row:- Amanda Hughes, Lesley Walker, Melanie Cheshire, ?.?, Dawn Powell, Kevin Price, Shaun Connolly, Jessica Veysey, ?.?, Sara Smith and ?.?. Third Row:- ?.?, Michelle George, Julie Hodges, Ellen Hodges, Diana Keeble, ?. Keeble, Jayne Angel, and ?.?. Front:- Carl Hobbs and Simon Hickman.

87. Mr. Henley Ackland and class at Tynewydd Junior School, 1973. Headmaster M. Lloyd Griffiths is on the left. Back Row, left to right:- Mark Bolwell, Timothy Shepherd, Stuart Griffiths, Alun Thoms, Christopher Smith, Christopher Leader, Keith Herbert, and Neil Pfeiffer. Second Row:- Elizabeth Collins, Joyce Edmunds, Janet Griffiths, Mary Breeze, Lesley Johnson, Julie Hawkins, Tracey Salvidge, Theresa Gittings and Susannah Light. Third Row:- Christine Kinsey, Melanie Williams, Sharon Cook, Sheryl Wilkins, Louise Jones, Ceri-Anne Edwards, Keri Stephenson and Michelle Harvey. Front Row:- ?.?, Neil Davies, ?.?, Kevin Mason, Anthony Price and Christopher Hoskins.

88. Some of the staff and pupils at Newbridge Grammar School in 1947. Staff left to right:- Miss Hughes, Miss Williams, ?.?, ?.?, Miss Cecil, Mr. Cook, Headmaster, Mr. Talbot Thomas, Mr. Begbie, Mr. Halse and Mr. Davies.

89. Some staff and pupils at Newbridge Grammar School, 1973.
Staff left to right:- Mrs. B. James, Mrs. H. Jefferies, Miss S. Cecil, Dr. John Herbert, Mr. E. M. Jones, Mr. A. Bridgeman and Mr. H. Cowen.

90. Girls at Newbridge Grammar School, 1947.

91. Boys at Newbridge Grammar School, 1947.

92. An informal picture of boys from Form IV F at Newbridge Grammar School, 1955.

93. Standard 3 at Abercarn Girls School, c1907.

94. Miss Bowen's class at Gwyddon Infants School, Abercarn, c1953.

95. Pupils and staff at Gwyddon Secondary School, Abercarn, c1955. Teachers from left to right:- Mrs. Pritchard, Mrs. Davies, Mr. Phillips, (Headmaster), Mr. Rodway, Mr. Price, Mr. Davies and Mr. Langley.

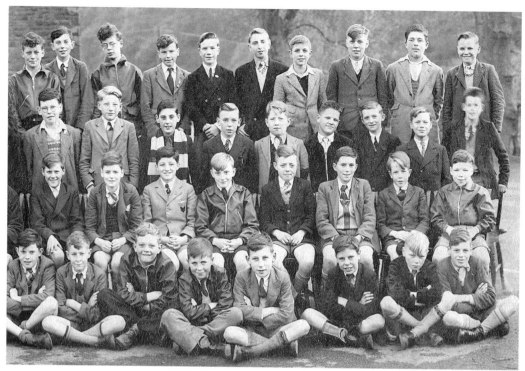

96. Some more pupils at Gwyddon Secondary School, c1955.

97. The Mayor of Islwyn Borough Council and Dignitaries at the unveiling of the memorial plaque to commemorate the opening of Ysgol Gymraeg Cwm Gwyddon, at Abercarn in 1992. The ceremony had been preceded by a play encompassing the lives of Lord and Lady Llanofer.

98. Mrs. Evans with her class at West End Junior School in 1956.

99. Staff at West End Junior School in the mid 1950s. Back Row, left to right:- Gordon Phillips, John Maiden, Gordon Davies, Mrs. Clarice Oliver, and Arnold Stephens. Front Row:- Mrs. Margaret Crowther, Mrs. Evans, Mr. Albert Stevens, (Headmaster), Miss Sheila Woodhouse, and Mrs. Olwen Kirkup.

100. Gordon Phillips and class at West End Junior School, 1966, with Headmaster Mr. Watkins to the right.

101. John Maiden with his class at West End Junior School, c1967.

102. Standard 2 at Cwmcarn Junior School in 1941. Back Row, left to right:- Miss Kate Simpson, Edith Watts, Mary Jones, Shirley Gay, Jan Veysey, Christine Huish, Pat Richards, ?.?, ?.?, Joan Taylor, ?. Davies. Second Row, left to right:- Vivian Morgan, Margaret Norman, Kathleen Roeberry, June Westcott, Pat Evans, Jean Hurford, ?. Pearce, ?.?, ?.?. Kneeling, left to right:- Gerald Morgan, Ray Carter, Horace Williams, Don Gogherty, Ron Wilton, Keith Davies, Chris Hillier. Seated, left to right:- Desmond MacDonald, Bill Tilley, Don Lane, ?.?, ?.?, Brian Hoskins, Jack Hurrell and John Russell.

103. Cwmcarn Junior School class group. Back Row, left to right:- Mr. Emery (Headmaster), Gerald Stroud, Jean Poole, Ann Jennings, Nancy Beard, Marion Jones, Barbara Jones, Doris Evans, Eileen Rideout, Harold Talbot, ?.?. Middle Row:- Arthur Gregory, Norman Taylor, Kitty Wyatt, Jenny Dight, Norma Cox, Eileen Weetch, Shirley ?, Stan Bigham Miss/Mrs ? Front Row:- Ithel Whatley, Noel Hopkins, Don Sayce, ?.?, Gwyn Haynes, ? Veysey, ?.?, ? Hawkins, ? Williams, and Granville Maggs.

104. Miss Glenys Barnes with her class at Cwmcarn Infants School in the early 1940s.

105. Miss Glenys Barnes with her entrants' class at Cwmcarn Infants School, c1951. To the right is Miss Davies, the Infants School Headmistress.

106. Class Group at Cwmcarn Junior School, c1974, with Headmaster Mr. Gordon Davies, and their supply teacher.

107. Class Group at Cwmcarn Junior School, c1975, with Headmaster Mr. Gordon Davies and Miss Ida Stephens.

108. An informal group of Juniors (photographed in the Infants yard) at Cwmcarn School, June 1960. Back Row, left to right:- Grayson Blakemore, Kelvin Dark, Steven Harlin, and Stephen Crockett. Front Row, left to right:- Brian Dawkins, Stephen Fiddler, Dennis Gilbert, Peter Maiden, Granville Pitman and Phillip Smith.

109. Staff at Cwmcarn Junior School, c1970. Back Row, left to right:- Mrs. Barbara Collins, Mrs. Iris Percy, (Secretary), Mrs. Lynne Hawkins and Miss Capers. Front Row:- Mrs. Glynis Williams, Miss Ida Stephens, Mr. Gordon Davies, (Headmaster), Mrs. Muriel Dudley and Mr. John Attwood.

110. An Infants class at Crosskeys 'Old School', 1968, with Headmaster Mr. Bill Tilley, and Teacher Miss Mary Lewis.

111. Staff at Waunfawr Junior and Infants School, Crosskeys, c1980. Back Row, left to right:- Phillip Banfield, Mrs. Christine Ransome, Mrs, Jeanette Knight, Mrs. Hodges (School Secretary), and Maurice Thomas. Front Row:- Mrs. Ann Brelsford, Miss Audrey Coleman, Mr. John Maiden, (Head Teacher), Mrs. Jean Thomas and ?.?.

112. Celebrating the Centenary of Waunfawr School, with Headmaster Mr. Paul Fowler and the first Mayor of Caerphilly County Borough, Mrs. Carol Sadler.

113. Class group at Risca Town School, c1970. Back Row, left to right:- Michael Dunn and Nicholas Suter. Middle Row:- Wayne Perkins, Beverley Green, Kay Jones, Julie Jeffries, Cherry Wilton, Lynne Guy, Gaynor Slocombe, Martin Richards, Mark Harris and Mr. Battle. Front Row:- Sally-Anne Evans, Linda Lewis, Tracey Barrow, Lynne Harris, Sally-Anne Graham, Julie Munn, Marie Harries and Sharon Hall.

114. The Risca Town British System School opened in March 1850. It was later to be called simply Risca Town School.

115. Removal of the old school has made way for the residential development of Cwrt Yr Ysgol.

116. Teachers at Ty Sign Junior School, c1970, with Headmaster Mr. Ronald Lewis.

117. John Maiden's class at Ty Sign Junior School, 1971-72, with Headmaster Mr. Ronald Lewis on the left. Back Row, left to right:- Reeves Wilfred, Mark Wiltshire, Gary Salmon, Mark O'Neill, Paul Jones, Neil Milton, Richard Gibb and Neil Barker. Middle Row:- Karl Pendry, David Combstock, Paul Oliver, Stephen Lloyd, Dean Grey, David Stokes, and Stephen Peacock. Front Row:- Owen Williams, Angharad Edwards, Margaret Basson, Siân Bowen, Kerry Cook, Julie Saroby, Linda Bourne, Andrew Smith and Christopher Bishop.

118. Class Group at Dan-y-Graig Junior School, Risca, c1940. Back Row, left to right:- Royston Evans, Ivor Griffiths, Abner Jenkins, Noel Lewis, and Derek Gregory. Second Row:- Leonard Whitcombe, Billy Harris, John Rounds, Alan West(?), and Graham Ward. Third Row:- Jimmy Jenkins, John Shepherd, Stan Prothero, Howard Woodberry, John Alan, ? James, Reg Hatherall and David Duffield. Fourth Row:- Norah Gundy, Bernice Jones, Moira Davies, Barbara Williams, Susan Tutton, Doris Nash, and Pauline Hodges. Front Row:- Michael Gregory, Jean Martin, Maureen Mattock, Marion Pook, Mary Shepherd, Ann Padfield and Tony Martin.

119. Pontywaun County School was constructed by Jno. Pritchard of Risca. The foundation stone was laid with great ceremonial by Lord Tredegar in August 1899, and the opening ceremony took place on 2nd November 1900. The title of the School later became Pontywaun County Grammar School, and it closed in 1963. The site has been developed to provide an Adult Training Centre.

120. Form 2 at Pontywaun County Grammar School in 1961. Back Row, left to right:- Peter Lloyd, Peter Glastonbury, Derwin Pratley, Stephen Phillips and Roy Gilbert. Middle Row:- Colin Hawkins, Robert Dark, Noel Smith, Sam Lewis, David Davies, Janice ?, Lorna Regan, Elaine Harris, Pat Simpkins, Andrea Gittings, Jeffrey Davies, Judith Havard, Martin Power, Keith Phillips, Steven Thomas, Clive Jones and Russell Sims. Front Row:- Hazel Smith, Susan Parry, Judith Robbins, Janet Vowles, Kate Lawrence, (Form Teacher), Linda Whittington, Maureen Benham, Magda Kaminski and Margaret Rideout.

Chapter 4

Religion

121. Choir at St. Mary's Church, Crumlin. The Church building began life as a school, a prominent feature being the bell high up on the front wall. Structural problems, together with the cost of having to provide access and facilities for the disabled, and a dwindling membership led to its closure. Services were held at the Old Age Pensioner's Centre in Crumlin Square for a while, but now the congregation has merged with that of the Parish Church, St. Paul's, in Newbridge.

122. Members of Zion Congregational Church, Newbridge, taking part in the Whitsun March of 1959. The Church became Zion United Reformed Church in 1966, and closed in 2006.

123. Choir at St. Paul's Church, Newbridge, 1963.

124. Zion Congregational Church in Newbridge had its beginnings in Golden Grove, (the 'Old Zion' chapel now being occupied by the Pentecostal Church), before moving to High Street. In 1966 Zion became a United Reformed Church, but dwindling numbers led to its closure in December 2005.

125. Zoah Congregational Church was opened in the early part of the twentieth century to satisfy the needs of the Welsh speaking members of Zion. The Chapel was located at the lower end of Park Hill.

126. Wesley Hall, Newbridge, erected in 1921 to replace the Methodist Chapel in Golden Grove, (now part of the Pentecostal's Mission Hall). The old army building was obtained as a temporary measure, but it remained in use until the present chapel was opened in 1952. The old timber hall still exists and is used for commercial purposes.

127. St. Luke's Church Choir, Abercarn, with vicar Rev. Ray Summers.

128. Construction work on the main entrance during the building of St. Luke's Church, Abercarn, in 1923.

129. An impressive floodlit view of the Church, which has since become derelict. St. Luke's congregation now worships at the nearby Welsh Church.

130. A procession, which started at the old Tin Church in West End, approaching St. Luke's in Abercarn on the occasion of its fortieth anniversary in 1966.

131. The Methodist Chapel, Commercial Road, Abercarn, from an original painting by Obediah Hodges, 1907. The Chapel was built in 1886.

132. Nazareth Chapel, Cwmcarn, from an original drawing by local artist and poet Elizabeth Leach. The Presbyterian Chapel was one of the oldest in the area, built in 1841, and rebuilt in 1891.

133. A group outside Nazareth Chapel in the early 1950s.

134. Celebrating Shrove Tuesday, c1970, with a pancake race at St. John's Church, Cwmcarn, with Vicar Rev. Ken Davies. Contestants from left to right:- Barbara Jones, Terry Birt, Barbara Jones, Barbara Evans, Gwyneth Nash, Christine Powell, Pat Wilkins and Sylvia Charlottes. Winner on that occasion was Barbara Jones on the extreme left.

135. St. John's Whitsun Marchers seen in John Street, Cwmcarn, in 1966.

136. Crosskeys Methodist Church Officers c2000. Left to right:- Michael Gray, John Prosser, Rev. Soba Sinnathamby, Brian Hamer and Len Chivers.

137. Ladies' group at Crosskeys Pentecostal Church in the mid 1930s, with Pastor Tom Mercy.

138. Whitsun March passing along Risca Road, Crosskeys, c1980, led by John Prosser and Francis Jenkins.

139. Zoah Calvinistic Methodist Church, St. Mary Street, Risca. The Chapel was built in 1860, after use was made of Soar Cottages nearby. It was demolished in 1990 when the congregation joined Dan-y-Graig Church.

140. The earliest Methodist Church in the district was at Colliery Place, on the west bank of the river Ebbw. The congregation was to be divided into the Wesleyan section and the Primitive Methodists. The Wesleyans were soon to move to an alternative location, and the remaining Primitive Methodists were forced to vacate the Chapel at Colliery Place after it was badly damaged by flooding. This led to the construction, in 1893, of both a Chapel and a separate Sunday School on Grove Road, Risca, shown above.

141. Ebenezer was closed in 1963, and has since been used for different commercial purposes at the junction of St. Mary Street with Grove Road. The picture, taken in March 2007, shows the main building to be relatively unchanged outwardly, but that the Sunday School has been replaced by a more functional structure.

142. Group at Fernlea Pentecostal Church which was opened in 1948. With dwindling numbers, and continual vandalism, the Church was closed in 1998, and the building demolished in April 1999.

143. A production of Noah at the first Sunday School Anniversary of the new Dan-y-Graig Church in 2001.

Chapter 5

Sport & Leisure

144. Crumlin Cricket Club, c1970. Back Row,, left to right:- R. J. Lewis, A. Powell, S. J. Williams, G. Taylor, A. Rhodes, C. Barrett, A. G. Davies and C. Daunter. Front Row:- K. Daniel, (standing), B. Williams, R. Morgan, L. Cheshire, (Captain), R. Shepherd and P. Fox.

145. Crumlin Cricket Club, 1976. Back Row, left to right:- T. Hatherall, S. Williams, C. Daunter, A. Roberts, R. Lewis, D. Noris, B. Bartley, C. Coombes and L. Cheshire. Middle Row:- P. Shepherd, M. Miles and S. Williams. Front Row:- S. Shepherd, G. Davies, (Captain), J. Evans, (Vice Captain), and A. James.

146. Crumlin Rugby Football Club, A side Champions 1998-99 Back Row, left to right:- Andrew Chess (Coach), Gary Hewlett (Coach), Stuart Shepherd, Christian Jones, Lee Pearce, Lee Morgan, Martin Valcic, Paul Fry, Simon Lloyd, Jonathan Pritchard, Paul Brayley, Jason Hopkins, David Hicks, Vaughan Jenkins and Arthur Lewis. Front Row:- David Hobden, Rob Phillips, Paul Pearce, Dean Parfitt (Captain), David Alexander, Kevin Phelps, Craig Williams and Terry Noel.

147. Crumlin Rugby Football Club, Season 1986-87, in which they reached the final of the Ben Francis Cup. Back Row, left to right:- D. Williams, (Coach), A. D. Richards, (Secretary), M. Jenkins, S. Penn, C. Hobbs, L. Cox, S. Irwin, G. Levy, J. Jones, M. Taylor, M. Valcic and R. Taylor, (Trainer). Middle Row:- J. Davies, M. Jones, P. Morgan, (Captain), B. Doman and C. Lewis. Front Row:- K. Doman and A. Davis.

148. Newbridge Under-Eleven Rugby Team, 1980. All but Andrew Nash went on to play senior rugby for Crumlin. Standing, left to right:- Andrew Ryan, Mike Shallish, John Fox, Paul Shipp and Garrod Musto. Seated:- Dean Stevens, Darren Jones, Phillip Jones, Jason Tavener and Andrew Nash.

149. The outdoor swimming baths at Chapel of Ease, Abercarn, were constructed during the Depression, employing men who were otherwise out of work. (The other similar pool in the locality was at Risca, at the back of the Long Bridge field). Outdoor leisure facilities are fine when the weather is favourable. On those occasions the baths were over popular, resulting in 'sessions'. Queues formed outside the entrance for up to two hours or more, when those already inside were hastily directed to the changing areas and required to leave.

Bathers at Chapel of Ease will remember how welcome chunks of bread were, when purchased from an enterprising shopkeeper just up the road.

150. After a few years, there developed a demand for leisure facilities in the area. Leisure Centres were built at Cwmcarn in 1975, and at Risca in 1978, both being shared with the adjacent schools. The Centre at Newbridge followed in 1984, sharing its facilities with the Comprehensive School and the local community.

Many changes however have taken place since its inception. A pair of squash courts were added the following year, with two squash clubs adopting the Centre as their home base - the Newbridge Squash Club still does.

In 1996, an artificial turf pitch was acquired together with an impressive pool which was designed by the Gwent County Council Architect, Gillian Jewel. It is still claimed to be the best in the Caerphilly Borough. Facilities associated with the pool include flumes, a boat, a bubble bath, water cannons and sprays, adding much to its popularity. The flume requires a climb of about ten metres to its entrance, sliding down to the water in about ten seconds. Very well attended swimming lessons provide a valuable service to the users of the pool.

A fitness suite was introduced to the Centre in 1998. Prior to this time, a weights room existed in what was once a broom cupboard in a building nearby. Several extensions later, the Centre has one of the largest fitness suites in the area, with the newest refurbishment and brand new equipment being installed for Christmas 2006. With new state-of-the-art equipment, it is set to rival private gyms such as the likes of David Lloyd and Fitness First.

(Sean Spooner, Manager, Newbridge Leisure Centre)

151. Newbridge Welfare Cricket Team, 1964. Back Row, left to right:- D.Weare, W. Harris, R. Coleman, R. Britten, M. Jones, T. Leader, B. Porter, L. Veysey, K. Jones, G. Charles, P. Britten, H. Vowles and ?.?. Middle Row:- G. Jones, ?.?., R. Simmonds, H. Watkins, E. Cooper, L. Rowlands and J, Britten. Front Row:- W.R. Watkins, R. Woodford, R. Meredith, E. James, D. Jones, B. Clark, D. Hughes, R. McQuilliam and J. Evans .

152. Newbridge Grammar School Cricket 1st Eleven, 1950. Back Row, left to right:- Arthur Harris, Keith Thomas, Jim Elliot, Russell Strong (Scorer). Middle Row:- Norman Burton, Brian Wellington, Colin Deneen, Billy Watkins. Front Row:- John Stanley, David Hayward, Brian Crewe, and Glyn Jandrell.

153. Newbridge Grammar School Rugby team, 1948-49. Back Row, left to right:- John Elliot, John Morgan, Barrie Nichols, John Jenkins, Peter Janes, Glanville Phelps, Norman Morgan, Ken Richards, Alan Smith (Touch Judge). Middle Row:- Mr. Talbot Thomas, David Hayward, Percy Hughes (Captain), Mr. A.T.S. Cooke, (Headmaster), Brian Vincent, Bill Thomas, Mr. Idris Roberts. Front Row:- Don James, Billy Watkins, Stuart Hughes, and Peter Burton.

Dai Hayward and Billy (Mousie) Watkins were later to gain Senior Welsh International honours.

154. One of the finest and most successful boxers in British history, Joe Calzaghe, was born in Hammersmith in 1972, but has lived in Newbridge for most of his life. His mother Jackie, being from Markham, meant the family moving to South Wales when he was 2 years of age. Joe began boxing at the age of nine, and turned professional in 1993, two years later being voted Young Boxer of the Year by the Professional Boxing Association and the Boxing Writers Club. By the end of that year he had become British Champion. Now managed by Frank Warren, he is the current WBO and former IBF Super Middleweight World Champion. His record to date speaks for itself. Total fights 43, Wins 43, Wins by KO 32, with 20 defences of his World Super Middleweight Title. In 2006, Joe was named the BBC's Sports Personality of the Year.

155. His inspiration and trainer is his effervescent Italian father Enzo, who has also passed on his undoubted skills to several other Welsh Boxers. Enzo was named by The Ring magazine as the 2007 Trainer of the Year.

156./157. Joe's base for a number of years was at the Newbridge Boxing Club (left) at Newbridge Welfare Ground. It had previously been used as changing rooms for Newbridge rugby and soccer teams. For safety and health reasons the building was condemned by the local

authority and pulled down in 2002. He continued his training at the Cwmcarn Boxing Club, (in the old British Legion Hall), for a while before moving to newer premises.

The current 'Newbridge Boxing Club' (right) is actually located at Abercarn Welfare Ground, and was originally the clubhouse of Cwmcarn United Rugby Football team.

Other outstanding boxers, benefiting from Enzo's training environment at the Newbridge club, include Gary Lockett, WBU Middleweight Champion, Enzo Macarinelli, WBO Cruiserweight Champion, and Bradley Pryce, Commonwealth Light Middleweight Champion and Gavin Rees, WBA World Light Welterweight Champion.

158. Pictured left at the Newbrige Club are Joe and Enzo Maccarinelli, after completing a gruelling training routine in May 2007.

159. John Dawes being carried off the pitch at Cardiff Arms Park in 1973 following the famous win by the Barbarians over New Zealand. It was his last International rugby match. Born at Chapel of Ease, John was educated at Gwyddon School, Lewis School Pengam and Aberystwyth University. His prowess in rugby led to captaincy, and later coach, of the British Lions.   (© *Western Mail*)

160. An Abercarn table tennis team, c1950, displaying proof of their winning ways, the photograph being taken in the grounds of the Miners' Institute. Back Row, left to right:- ? ?, ? ?, ? ?, Ken Venn, and Ken Brown. Front Row: David Thomas and Harold Wilkins.

161. Abercarn Ladies' Bowls Club, 1990, being the first year of affilation to the South Wales and Monmouthshire County Association. Back Row, left to right:- Betty Jones, Barbara Allen, Zoe Silverthorne, Grace Beechey, Kath Dyer, Muriel Court, Joyce Price-Stephens, Gladys Haywood, Barbara Phillips, Brenda James, Peggy Jones, Nancy Jones, Marjorie Evans, and Betty Dent. Front Row:- Glenys Hodges, Mary Charles, Maureen Driscoll, Claire Davies, Jean Ives, Peggy Hale, Min Evans, Dilys Williams and Karen Pewtner. Foreground:- Eileen Matthews, (President), and Jean Silverthorne, (Captain). The Ladies Club was founded in 1989.

162.   An interesting picture of the founder of the scouting movement, Robert Baden Powell, being photographed at a Jamboree in 1936. The Abercarn Group's resresentative, on that occasion, Ron 'Lofty' Smith is seen on the extreme left.

The then Monmouthshire County was well to the forefront in establishing a number of scout troops, one of the first being the 1st Risca, where it is recorded that L. Driscoll became Scout Master there in 1909. By 1910 there were as many as eight scout troops in the County that took part in a Church Parade together with members of the Church Lads Naval Brigade and Territorial Cadets, the parade being addressed by Colonel Arthur Mackworth, C.B.

During the period from when the first troops were formed, Risca had registered three other troops by 1927 as did the Newbridge troop whose first Scout Master was E. Burris in 1912. The 2nd Newbridge troop, which was registered in 1932, was in fact a Rover Crew which was for older lads, but only had a short existence due to the sudden death of a young leader. The 3rd Newbridge Group being the current group was joined in an amalgamation by the 4th Newbridge in 1949.

The other troop in the close locality was the 1st Pontywaun which was first registered around 1925, with the Scout Master George Howell, who later became District Commissioner of the Abercarn and District Association.

Up until the middle of the 1930s most, if not all of the then scout groups would have been using the likes of Church halls etc as their meeting places, before grants from the King George VI funds were made available for them to build their own scout huts. The design of these was of a wooden construction, mainly built on a parcel of land given to them by wealthy land owners.

The Newbridge Hut was built at the rear of what was then the Grand Cinema, where their present rebuilt Headquarters still stands on ground given by Lady Llanofer. The Abercarn Hut was situated on the parcel of land between what was then the Salvation Army Church and Foxon's Garage on the side of the Monmouthshire Canal. The Pontywaun Hut was officially opened by the County Commissioner, the Rt Hon Lord Raglan JP, on February 25th 1939. This particular hut, which is situated at the end of Halls Road Terrace in Pontywaun, is still essentially the same as the original structure.

163. Abercarn Group Leaders outside their newly built hut in 1938. In the distance to the left, over the canal and above the retaining wall, is seen part of the Social Centre building.

In 1977, The Scout District of Islwyn made a major step forward in providing its groups with a facility to spend more time outdoors - by way of Islwyn Scout Parc. A piece of land adjacent to Pantyscawen Farm in Newbridge was purchased for a permanent campsite. Monies to buy this were raised by a sponsored 48 hour run around the Oakdale recreation ground. A gateway and an obelisk were erected on which all the groups within the Islwyn District were named, together with a tablet commemorating the opening in June 1978 by the Chief Scout Sir William Gladstone, grandson of the famous Prime Minister.

Further changes occurred nationally, when in the late 1980s girls were allowed to join the previously all male domain of Venture Scouting, then eventually working through all the other sections to include both sexes. A number of years later the new section of Beaver scouts was introduced allowing 6 to 8 year olds to become members of the World Wide Scouting Movement.

In the late 1990s a Lottery Grant for £111,000 was obtained to construct an activity centre. After completion, the Chief Scout William Garth Morrison officially opened this aspect of Islwyn Scout Parc on 4th December 1999. Apart from the local usage the Scout Park enjoys, it has become a truly international attraction for Scouting and other organisations that require similar character-building training.

164. Islwyn District Commissioner, Reg Dowden, expressing thanks to Major General Michael Walsh, Chief Scout, for officially opening the new District Headquarters in May 1983.

(Reg Dowden, Islwyn District Commissioner, 1981 to 2000)

165. Abercarn Rugby Team, Captain Les Shipp, winners of the Ben Francis Cup in 1978, beating Garndiffaith 4-0. The match was played at Newbridge Welfare Ground.

166. Abercarn Rugby Team, 1949. Several of those in the photograph lost their lives the following year in the Llandow Air Disaster.

167. Officers and Committee of Abercarn Rugby Football Club, 1962-63.

168. Abercarn Cricket Club 1948-49. Back Row, left to right:- ?.?., Leighton Davies, Bill Sage, ?.?., ?.?., ? Millard, ?.?., Oliver Thorne, and ?.?. Middle row:- Melville Bray (umpire), Ray Taylor, Harold Wilkins, Randolph Harries, Ray Edwards, Jack Jones, Mel Bray, ?.?., Ken Brown, Marsden Barnes and Ray Bevan, (umpire). Front Row:- John Lewis, Curnow Coleman, Cyril Thornbury, Horace Lewis, (Captain), Llewellyn Francis, Alf White and David Thomas.

169. Abercarn Cricket team 1970. Back Row, left to right:- David Owens, Maldwyn Nash, Chris Browning, Bob Charles, John Tidmarsh, Cyril 'Titch' Hopkins and John Sellick. Front Row:- Garfield Johnson, Glyn Meredith, Don Williams, Curnow Coleman, Jack Loughman, David Lewis, and Trevor Hopkins.

170. Abercarn Cricket Club Dinner in the early 1950s. Back Row, left to right:- Ray Foley, Harold Wilkins, Jack Loughman, Graham Wilton, Lyndon Jones, Roger Foley, Len Morgan, Rosser Watkins, Jack Jones, Ron Moses, David Thomas and Garfield Johnson. Middle Row:- Dai Lewis, Terry Long, Ivor Burnett, Cyril Hopkins, Don Harris, Roy Sykes, John Sellick, Ray Edwards and John Lewis. Front Row:- Mrs. Marie Prout, Albert Prout, Oliver Thorne, Bill Sage, Dr. Adam Buick, S. Davies, Ray Taylor, Horace Lewis and Curnow Coleman.

171. Cwmcarn Paragon Cycling Club was founded in 1932, the first General Meeting being held at the premises of Messrs Grist, Newport Road on 17th October 1933. The meeting was attended by 23 members, who elected T. J. Thompson as Chairman, and T. J. Garland as Captain. The club grew in strength throughout the 1930s, building the first headquarters by May 1936, at Brooklands at the bottom of Factory Trip, Cwmcarn. The club remained steady throughout the war years. Then, in 1947, the success rate began with riders such as Trevor West, Jack James, Jack Hatfield, and the Carpenter brothers Ted and Mel winning many Welsh records and championships on road and track. In 1948 Ted Harrhy became the first to win all four Welsh track championships in one year, the quarter mile, the half mile, the one mile

and the five miles. The successes continued throughout the 1950s and the 1960s, and in 1970 John Hatfield was selected to represent Wales at the Commonwealth Games in Edinburgh, where he won the bronze medal in the 1000 metres tandem sprint, and was then selected to represent Great Britain in the World Championships. In 1974 he was selected as captain of the cycling team, and was the flag bearer to lead the Welsh team out at the Commonwealth Games in Christchurch, New Zealand. In 1976 the club members demolished the old clubroom and built the new one, which is there today. 1986 saw Mark Westwood selected for the Commonwealth Games, again held in Edinburgh. The 1990s heralded the beginning of mountain bikes, and of the club becoming sponsored, resulting in a large increase in membership, and successes with the club winning just about every event in the calendar. 1993 saw Paul Sheppard win the British juvenile pursuit title, and Tim Williams the British youth mountain bike downhill title. Tim then represented Great Britain in the World Championships in 1995 in Germany, and in 1996 in Australia. He also won the British downhill title, with Paul Shepard taking the British Junior 20 kilometre title, and Megan Hughes the bronze medal in the junior ladies World Sprint Championship in the USA. By 1998 the membership had increased to over 120, and five members, Paul Sheppard,

172. Cwmcarn Paragons Pursuit Team, Welsh Champions in 1948 at Grovesend Welfare Ground. Left to right:- Jack Hatfield, Cedric Hall, John Waring and Ted Harrhy.

Chris Williams, Paul Esposti, Anthony Malarczyk and Megan Hughes, were selected to represent Wales at the Commonwealth Games held at Kuala Lumpur. 2002 saw Paul Sheppard and Anthony Malarczyk selected for the Commonwealth Games held in Manchester, and in 2005 Anthony Malarczyk took the gold medal in the British cross-country mountain bike championships. The future of the club looks very healthy with fresh young talent such as Andrew Williams, Sam Harrison, Matthew Jones, and Jack Llewellyn already winning Welsh titles.

(John Hatfield)

173. Surmounting one of the hurdles in a cyclo-cross race around The Graig, at Cwmcarn, in the early 1950s.

174. Cwmcarn Paragons' Bicycle Polo team, photographed at Waunfawr Park in the mid 1940s. Bert Carlton, Wally Garland, Johnny Hart, Tom Watkins, Cliff Garland and Johnny Werin.

175. Cwmcarn Athletic Under Elevens Soccer Team, 1968. Back Row, left to right:- David Elseley, (Coach), Paul Turner, Ian Vines, Keith Jones, Mike Banwell, Jeremy Thomas, Robert Matthews. Front Row:- Martin Turner, Martin Madden, Peter Butcher, Paul Daniel, Lyndon Ryall, Stephen Perkins and Keiron Spencer.

176. Cwmcarn Comprehensive School Hockey Team, c1973.

177. Cwmcarn United Rugby team, 1954-55. Back Row, left to right:- Jack Alford, Jack Hillier, Bill Evans, Peter Shropshall, Norman Hillier and Glanville Phelps. Middle Row:- Alan Williams, Cy Beechey, George Rossiter (Captain), Tom Davies and Keith Colebrook. Front Row:- John Tidmarsh, Clive Wilks, Fred Lewis, Roy Churcher, Don Jones and ?. ?.

178. Successive generations made their own fun by damming the River Carn, or the brook as it was affectionately known, opposite Feeder Row in Cwmcarn. The picture shows one such pond in the early 1930s. The embankment of the railway serving Cwmcarn Colliery is seen in the background. Many local people, including the author, learned to swim at this location, ably taught by their peers.

179. Schoolmaster and successful billiards player L.G. (Lou) Barnes of Pontywaun, winner of the British Legion Championship in 1935.

Being proficient at billiards was often quoted as being 'a sign of a misspent youth'. This certainly was not true in Mr. Barnes's case as he also became a successful academic.

He was a regular at Staite's Billiards Hall on Factory Trip, as was another accomplished player, Royden Jandrell.

Before the successful BBC programme Pot Black, snooker took second place to billiards in this part of the world, with facilities being available at the Miners' Institutes, as well as at private establishments such as Staite's.

The valley has since seen some highly ranked snooker professionals, such as Doug Mountjoy, Darren Morgan, (see page 99), and Leigh Walker.

As in most sports, highly skilled amateurs of those early days might well have lived different lifestyles, had today's opportunities been available.

180. Darts team of the Castle Inn, Pontywaun, in the mid 1940s. Holding the dartboard was Charlie Parker, at one time Welsh Champion.

181. Darren Morgan is a highly successful local sportsman. He developed his skills at the Red Triangle Snooker Club in Crosskeys. He represented his country as an amateur, and in 1987 won the Welsh Amateur Championship. The photograph opposite shows his jubilant return in 1987 from Bangalore India after winning the World Amateur title. He soon afterwards turned professional and rose to his highest position of eighth in the world rankings. Darren won six professional titles which included the Pontin's Professional title both in 1989 and 2000, the Welsh Professional title in 1990 and again in 1991, the International one-frame knockout, now known as Pot Black, in 1991, and his biggest win came in 1996 in taking the Irish Benson and Hedges Masters championship, defeating his favourite player Steve Davies. Darren also went on to captain the Welsh team to success in the 1999 Nations Cup, when beating the favourites Scotland in the final. Having now retired from the professional circuit, he has become the proud owner of the Red Triangle Snooker Club, and is putting a great deal back into the sport by running a very successful junior section. Many promising youngsters are being encouraged to take part in competitions and in league teams. Competing again as an amateur, Darren has recently won both the Welsh and the European Masters Titles.

182. Some of the prize winners at the Junior Presentation at the Red Triangle club in September 2003. Trophies were presented by Mark Williams, front left, who, at the time, was World Champion, and ranked as World Number One. The World Cup is held by Christian Bishop to the front right.

183. Crosskeys Bowls Club - Monmouthshire Runners Up in 1958. Back Row, left to right:- P. Martin, W. Strange, V. Beacham, K. Venn and E. Hawkins. Middle Row:- G. Evans, C. Hurn, A. Jones, H. Pembro, J. Betty, C. Evans and G. Ashman. Front Row:- S. Crewe, G. Durban, H. Benger, H. Ashworth, J. Morris, E. Whatley and H. Hart.

184. Crosskeys Bowls Club - Monmouthshire Champions in 1975. Back Row, left to right:- J. Slade, L. Morgan, P. Trinder, G. Trinder, M. Howells and R. Kenvyn, Second Row:- D. Watkins, F. Williams, P. Kane, I. Tilley, L. Kemp, K. Trinder and G. Williams. Third Row:- C. Evans, E. Banfield, J. Betty, A. Rowe and K. Venn. Front Row:- G. Forward, C. Hurn, D. Howells, L. Ashman, P. Richards and W. Jeffries.

185. Crosskeys Cricket Club 1st XI, 1989. Back Row, left to right:- D. Tucker, M. Brown, R. Morgan, B. Jones, S. Mayers, N. Thompson and S. Cullen. Front Row:- P. Haynes, L. Kembery, M. Jenkins (Captain), P. Jenkins and M. Baker.

186. Crosskeys Cricket Team, 1995, Newport and District Freeguard Cup Winners. Back Row:- G. Davy, M. Baker, G. Morgan, R. Evans, K. Mellish and D. Clements. Front Row:- G. Rees, D. Rees, C. Evans, I. Collier, (Captain), G. Evans and C. Jones.

187. Crosskeys United Rugby players following their invincible season 1949-50. Back Row, left to right:- Walter Moon, Ron James, John Herrera, Malcolm Quartley, Dick Burnett, Arthur Tremlett, Lawson Haines, Albert Bridgeman. Second Row, left to right:- Glyn Whatley, Mervyn Deneen, Ray Beechey, Billy Rowe, Ron Gundy, Don Lewis, Ray Parfitt. Third Row, left to right:- Delwyn Morris, Don Green, Roy Dutton, Garnett Tyrrell (captain), Royce Moon, Malcolm Whatley, Lyndon Smith. Front Row, left to right:- Don Evans, Gwyn Speed, Geoff Parsons, Jack Legge, Gordon Parry and Brian Padfield.

188. Crosskeys Youth Rugby Football Club, 1966-67. Back Row, left to right:- Don Evans, David Thomas, Robert Harry, Michael Phillips, Les Thomas, Graham Harvey, Paul Shepherd, John House, Bryn Thomas, Brian Mills and ? Lewis. Second Row:- Robert Oliver, Andrew Noakes, Alan Davies, Chris Evans and Sam Lewis. Front Row:- Mel Jones, Philip Silverthorne, Anthony Allen and Hugh Green.

189. Gordon Williams (centre) established Risca Garages Ltd., on Cromwell Road in 1955. He is seen here with his son Tony (right) and his stepson John Morgan, who successfully raced Jaguars in more than 600 events nationwide, over a period of some 25 years.

190. Gordon's younger son, Andy, has continued the family's racing tradition, becoming Welsh Saloon Car Champion in both 2005 and 2006.

191. Risca Town Junior School Football Team 1972. Back Row, left to right:- Mrs. Roberts, Mark Jerman, Martin Evans, Shaun Thomas, Carl Lugg and Mr. Bryn Charlottes, (Headmaster). Middle Row:- Colin Richards, Wayne Lewis, Jonathan Rowlands, Andrew Fido and Julian Hackling. Front:- Lee Jenkins and Robert Jones.

192. Risca United AFC team who won the Monmouthshire Senior League Challenge Cup in 1973. Back Row, left to right:- Lyn Rees, Jim Williams, Peter Hackling, Martin Perrett, Terry Peebles, Duncan Bartlett and Stuart Luckwell. Front Row: Kenny Kingston, John Powell, Howard Farley (Captain - with his young son), Gordon Ham and Derek Rees.

193. Jamie Baulch is another successful sportsman who was raised in the district. Growing up in a farm house with his parents, Alan and Marilyn, his brother and two sisters, Jamie being the youngest. The Baulch family was well known in the area with his grandfather, Arthur Baulch, being a well established businessman in Risca owning a funeral directors business. (see page 42)

Jamie soon established his status in the British Athletics team, having started his career at the age of 10. His junior school teacher recommended him to join a running club after seeing him run at the annual sports day. He joined Newport Harriers, and never looked back. It didn't take him too long to be noticed, and he moved up through the ranks, winning medals for Wales and Great Britain. In 1996, Jamie went to the Atlanta Olympics and came home with a silver medal for the 4x400 metres relay. His career lasted over a decade, winning a hoard of major medals, highlighted with a World Indoor gold medal in the individual 400 metres in Japan in 1999.

Jamie is a charismatic person, forging a career not just in track and field but also in television and media. He now has a successful media agency and sports management company.

194. Jamie Baulch, Mark Richardson, Iwan Thomas and Roger Black with their silver medals won in the 4 x 400-Metre Relay at the Olympics in Atlanta, 3 August 1996.

195. Risca Rugby Club, 1st. XV, 1968-69. Back Row, left to right:- M. Samuel, G. Thomas, J. Patrick, J. Evans, R. Morgan, A. Wilks, G. Huntley and A. Lewis. Middle Row:- R. Jeffries, A. Thompson, E. Friend (Captain), T. Shore and G. Humphries. Front Row:- L. Evans, M. James, N. Hunt and J. Parsons.

196. Risca Rugby Club, 1st XV, Monmouthshire League Premier Division Runners Up, 1986-87. Back Row, left to right:- M. James, K. Edmunds, C. Bateman, D. Williams, M. Jones, D. Bateman, A. Thompson, R. Bush, M. Harris and G. Bailey. Second Row:- G. Birch, S. Scott, P. Williams, P. Stokes, S. Brooks, R. Beale, A. Harding, C. Harding, J. Hill and M. Downs. Third Row:- P. Green, D. Williams, N. Griffiths, W. Orchard, S. Downs (Captain), J. James, S. Edwards, J. Gould and G. Lewis. Front Row:- M. Haytor, W. Jones, L. Tovey and P. Whatley.

197. Pontywaun County School Rugby team, c1936. Back Row extreme left is Sportsmaster Mr. Williams, and extreme right Headmaster Mr. Hughes.

198. Girls' cricket team at Pontywaun County School in 1945. Back Row, left to right:- Ellen Morton, Grace Harrhy, Marion Evans, Mrs. Mathias, Jean Morgan, Joyce ?, and Bernice Padfield. Front Row:- ? Knight, Margaret Knight, Freda Roberts, Mr. Lewis, (Headmaster), Susan Tutton, Josine Watkins and Josie Evans.

199. Pontymister Welfare Bowls Team, winners of the Carruthers Shield, 1947. Back Row, left to right:- G. Protheroe, I. Milsom, T. Jones, J. Chivers, A.T. Waites, L. Batt, J. Chivers, and W. Cook. Middle Row:- E. H. Milsom, W. Jones, J. James, H. Park, R.M. Morris, H.V. Taylor, B. Jones, T. Skinner and R. Elms. Front Row:- A.B. Williams, G. Benham, A.E. Evans, L.L. Taylor (Captain), F.C. Durban, I.T. Griffin and A.E. Porter.

200. Pontymister Welfare Bowls Club, winners of the Over Sixties League 1988 - Argus Shield. Back Row, left to right:- W. Everson, L. Rogers, H. Sayer, R. Roberts, S. Parker, D. Davies, B. Gibson, I. Whitcombe, T. Tutton, R. Thomas and G. Bosher. Front Row:- G. Ashman, V. Smith, T. Briffett, I. Jones, I. Davies, (Captain), S.T. Rogers and R. Oldhams.

201. Risca Leisure Centre, which is linked to Risca Comprehensive School, was opened, together with the school, by Her Majesty the Queen in June 1977, as part of her Silver Jubilee celebrations. The centre comprises outdoor courts and pitches, a six-court sports hall, a gymnasium, a 25-metre swimming pool, numerous function rooms, a café/bar area and the recently extended fitness suite. An artificial floodlit grass pitch was added to the outdoor area in 1997, and was officially opened by track athlete Jamie Baulch, a former pupil of Risca Comprehensive School. The Centre saw the arrival of an extended gymnasium six

years ago. The new facilities proved so popular that funding through the New Initiative fund was secured to build a second floor to the extension, and to make the reception area more welcoming and user friendly. This funding also covered the costs of the new equipment. The fitness suite includes eight running machines, seven cross trainers, eight stationary bikes, six rowing machines, a stepper, two hand bikes, and a range of weights equipment.

202. Over the years, the management and staff at Risca Leisure Centre have worked with Risca Comprehensive School to develop a programme that meets the needs of its local community and utilises the leisure centre to its maximum potential. Some of the clubs and activities on offer at the centre include, 'Risca Friends of the Heart' club, a mother and toddler group, pre and post-natal classes, junior gymnastics, yoga, hockey sessions and family evenings. The centre also offers a variety of swimming classes. The arrival of the new fitness suite has given the centre the opportunity to recruit seven new accredited fitness instructors who offer a wide range of services, including personal training, nutrition advice, cardiac rehabilitation and weight management counselling. The Centre is used for concerts, and it has been used for the International Football Festival, when the Centre played host to players from CCBC twinned regions. About 40 staff are employed, mainly from the local area, and membership currently stands at 230, but this figure continues to grow.

(John Ollman, Manager, Risca Leisure Centre)

203. Newport Rugby All International Team, 1962. Those named in italics were from the Crumlin to Pontymister area. Back Row, left to right:- G. Walters (Referee), *Des Greenslade*, Brian Creswell, Brian Price, Ben Edwards, Ian Ford, Geoff Whitsun, Glyn Davidge, and R. Taylor (Linesman). Middle Row:- *Gordon Britton*, Peter Rees, *Bryn Williams* (Club Chairman), Bryn Meredith, (Captain), Bill Everson (Hon. Secretary), *Brian Jones* and Norman Morgan. Front Row:- *Roy Burnett, Billy Watkins* and *Jack Hurrell.*

Chapter 6

Entertainment & Other Activities

204. Cow and Gate Carnival King Stan Reed with his Court at Kendon, Crumlin, c1947.

205. Members of Celynen Collieries Silver Band forming part of a carnival procession passing through Meredith Terrace, Newbridge, in the 1960s.

206. Celynen Collieries Silver Band, with Conductor Colin Radford, photographed at their then rehearsal room in Central Hall Abercarn, c1980. The band was re-formed in 1952, adopting numerous premises and several conductors over the years.

207. A group of locals meeting film star Gregory Peck at the time of the filming of *Arabesque* at Crumlin in 1965. His co-star was Sophia Loren.

208. Roger Pinney, Reporter for the BBC Wales Today programme, on location in Belarus in 2006, when he looked back at the 20th Anniversary of the Chernobyl nuclear accident. Roger moved to Newbridge at the age of five, after previously living in Crumlin and Cwmtillery. His father, Bill was manager of Crumlin Navigation Colliery. He has been in journalism all his working life. After graduating at Aberystwyth, he began with the Abergavenny Chronicle, then joined the South Wales Argus, before joining the BBC in 1986.

209. In 1898 a group of local miners formed themselves into a committee to establish an association aimed at improving the social amenities of their fellow workers. The original committee first met in the long room of the Beaufort Arms but soon moved moved to a coffee tavern in the village owned by the colliery company and the Celynen Collieries Welfare Scheme was born.

As Newbridge grew as a mining community the aspirations of the scheme grew too. Money was borrowed to build the Workmen's Institute. Opened in 1908 it provided a library, a snooker hall (with four tables), a reading room (with newspapers stocked daily) and various meeting rooms for the exclusive use of the miners and their dependants. To meet the running costs of the scheme every miner allowed two or three pence to be deducted from their already paltry wage packet every week. The Institute became the meeting place of the local Union and later the Miners Federation.

After the Great War of 1914-1918 it was decided that a fitting memorial was needed to honour the memory of those who fell. The Memorial Hall, built at a cost of £10,000, was opened in 1924 on a plot adjacent to the Institute. The building, soon known as the Memo, provided a cinema and stage on the upper floor, while the lower floor housed a dance hall and dressing rooms. This was a difficult period for the mining community and great use was made of the new facilities during the dark days of the Depression. Films were shown each night of the week except Sunday and dances were held two or three times a week and many events were held to raise funds for the out-of-work miners.

Immediately after the Second World War, Newbridge and the Memo became a centre for amateur drama in the region and regular drama competitions were held with the leading companies in South Wales and the West of England taking part. Celebrities of the time such as Donald Houston and Eynon Evans appeared on the stage in their own shows and at Christmas the children of the area were entertained with a pantomime. However the decline in cinema going started to take its toll in the 1960s and after a brief flirtation with bingo the Memo finally closed in 1972. In 1998 the magnificent art deco cinema was re-discovered by film producers and the Memo became the setting for two films *House* and *Very Annie Mary*. Unfortunately these productions caused even more damage to the original features of the building. The collieries which had been the basis for the development of the Welfare Scheme had all closed by 1985, and though the Institute attempted to continue as a club it was not viable and the buildings soon began to deteriorate, finally closing in 2003.

The prospect of completely losing this unique facility caused a group of local enthusiasts to form The Friends of Newbridge Memo under the chairmanship of Howard Stone, dedicated to saving the Institute and Memorial Hall (listed as Grade 2 by CADW in 2003). In 2004 the project was selected by the BBC for its Restoration programme and it won the Welsh section only to be narrowly beaten into second place in the UK final.

210. The work of The Friends came to the notice of HRH The Prince of Wales and in November 2006 he visited the Memo and pledged his support in helping to find the required funding for the restoration of the buildings. Meanwhile dances are once more being held, pantomimes performed and some fifteen different groups make use of the facilities whilst money is sought.

(Terry Powell)

211. An Abercarn based unit of the Home Guard, c1943. Private Pike has asked that no names be disclosed!

212. Members of the cast of *'Lollipop Land'*, performed at Park Hall, Cwmcarn, c1922.

213. Special guests at the Abercarn and Cwmcarn Carnival weekend in 1953 were Mr. And Mrs. J. Marriott, the Pearly King and Queen of London. They are seen here between Mr. Ivor Collins on the left, and Mr. Frank Edwards to the right. Proceeds from the carnival festivities that year benefited the Old Folks Xmas Fund, as always, but also the Abercarn R.F.C. Memorial Grand Stand Fund.

214./215. Carnival time at Cwmcarn in the 1950s. The annual event was always well supported, with a week of varied entertainment being organised by the committee. Proceeds helped to boost the Old Age Christmas Fund, providing the elderly of the district with welcome Christmas gifts.

216. A Christmas production at Cwmcarn Junior School in 1970. Standing, left to right:- Tim Maiden, Carl Doody, Siân Thomas, Jane Scott, Lisa Parsons, Clyde Poole, Maureen Dyer, Kevin Butcher, Jeremy Clarke. Kneeling, left to right:- Lee Oliver, Cienwen Rees, Stephen Perkins, Beverly Norville. Seated:- Robert Coles.

In the autumn of 1943 Ivor James, of Cwmcarn, a very talented and experienced musician, gathered together a group of local singers. He wanted to move away from the traditional male voice choir, the emphasis was to be on variety. Their accompanist was Eddie Williams who initially shared the musical direction with Ivor James. They needed a compere and a manager, their choice was Ivor Collins whose considerable organisation skills were used to good effect in making the name of the Dorian Singers known over a wide area. They gave their first concert in November 1943 and over the next ten years they travelled over most of Wales and much of England, they gave hundreds of concerts for a variety of good causes, they entered and won numerous competitions, appeared on radio, and were guest artists at offical dinners, prize-givings and receptions, and at the premiere of the film 'The Corn is Green' in Cardiff in 1947 they walked slowly onto the stage dressed as miners, pushing a tram of coal and singing an old Welsh folk song - versatile indeed!

The original Dorian Singers consisted of two sets of brothers - Horace and Larry Williams and Sam and Harold Morgan, Harry Watkins, Bryn Case, Percy Hughes, Will Clarke, Harold Morgan, and Tom Titley. Sometimes substitutes were needed for short or longer periods, these included Barrie Brooks, Bob Saunders, Ken Tiley and Jack Dent. The group's musical ability was remarkable, all were experienced choral singers who had competed successfully as soloists in eisteddfodau and other competitions, some of them - Horace Williams, Harry Watkins, Larry Williams, Bryn Case, Percy Hughes and Barrie Brooks - were regular 'Dorian' soloists. Later, accompanist Les Gay joined the group and shared the role with Eddie Williams. Musical arrangements were by Alec James, brother of conductor Ivor James.

The Dorian Singers appeared on 'Welsh Rarebit' and on two talent spotting programmes, 'The Carroll Levis Show' on BBC and 'Opportunity Knocks' on Radio Luxemburg, and were winners on both. Every Dorian Singers concert had a number of guest artists, one was a young soprano called Joan Roberts who later married Bryn Case, they toured with Carroll Levis and were billed as 'The Singing Sweethearts'. Percy Hughes and Barrie Brooks also joined Carroll Levis. Among the many singers, comedians, impressionists, solo musicians, conjurers and whistlers were Rosemary Jones, Doris Kingston, Eirewen Newberry, Joy Heatley, Marjorie Ralph, Gwen Williams, Gloria Powell, Barbara Davies, Les Gwynne, Teifion Thomas, Eddie Jones, Lionel Thomas and Bill Sewell (known as The Two Redheads), Doug Williams, Leslie James, Gomer Jones, Gordon Jenkins, Les Jones, Carl Bryant and Stan Stennett.

The highlight of the Dorian year was the concert they gave in Park Hall, Cwmcarn in aid of the local Christmas fund. They regarded it as the first concert of the coming season and always introduced some new musical items and sang old favourites too. This concert was hugely popular, tickets were in great demand and always sold out. The Dorian Singers disbanded in the early 1950s to the dismay of their many admirers, but the quality of their work and the pleasure they gave is still remembered.

Marjorie Maiden (nee Collins)

217. Left to right:- Horace Williams, Bob Saunders, Tom Titley, Ivor James (Musical Director), Joan Roberts (Soloist), Bryn Case, Larry Williams, Bill Clark, Eddie Williams, (Pianist), Harold Morgan, Harry Watkins, Sam Morgan and Ivor Collins, (Manager and Compere).

PARK HALL : CWMCARN

(KINDLY LENT)

SUNDAY, NOVEMBER 30th, 1947.

Abercarne & Cwmcarne Old Folks' Xmas Gift Fund

presents

The Dorian Singers

Conductor - - IVOR JAMES

in a popular programme of your favourite song arrangements.

ARTISTES :

TEIFION THOMAS (B.B.C.), The Golden Voice Boy Vocalist

ROSEMARY JONES, a new Soprano

BARRY BROOKS, The Sensational Young Baritone

LARRY WILLIAMS, Tenor, in his latest 'Songs from the Shows'

DORIS KINGSTON, an original Dorian Discovery

PERCY HUGHES (B.B.C.), the popular Carroll Levis Singer

GUEST STAR:

STAN STENNETT, late TERRY THOMAS' "STARS IN BATTLEDRESS."

Dorian Vocalists, Harry Watkins & Horace Williams.

The Voices in Harmony—Will Clarke, Sam Morgan, Harold Morgan and Tom Titley.

Compere - IVOR COLLINS (B.B.C.)

At the Piano - Eddie Williams & Leslie Gay.

Programme - - 3d.

J. R. Davies, Printer Abertillery

218.

219. Ken Parsons, and Glenys Barnes from Pontywaun, started dancing together in 1951. They married in 1952, and as amateurs they were undefeated South Wales and Welsh Champions. They won the Butlins Valeta Championship at the Royal Albert Hall in ???? The photograph to the left shows them being presented with the trophy by Billy Butlin himself.

In 1958 they were part of the Welsh team which won the BBC's Come Dancing final. Soon afterwards Ken and Glenys turned professional and became Isle of Man Professional Champions in 1963.

For many years they were responsible for the training of several successful dancers. They trained eight British Junior Champions, and in 1961 their Eight Couple Formation Team won the British Championship at the Winter Gardens Ballroom in Blackpool - see the photograph below.

After their dancing days, Ken and Glenys became judges at the highest level, participating in television's *Come Dancing*, and at the British Championships. In later years they were nominated for, and won, the Classique-de-Dance for the best sequence teaching. The nomination was made by their peers, indicating the esteem with which they were held within their profession.

Megan Loughman

220. The Parsons' Formation Dancing Team, after winning the Eight Couple Championship at the Winter Gardens, Blackpool in 1961.

221. Crosskeys Silver Band, 1982, with Musical Director Nigel Weeks. The band was formed in 1902 at the Primitive Methodist Church, taking in many of the members of an earlier colliery band, which went back to the opening of Risca North Colliery in 1871. The current rehearsal room is at Pandy Park. The band has achieved very many successes which the reader can find at www.crosskeysband.co.uk.

222. Risca Colliery Male Voice Choir, pictured in the Crosskeys Miners' Institute in the mid 1950s.

223. Crosskeys Youth Band, c1985, with Musical Director Robin Morgan. The Youth Band has again had many successes in local and national competitions and has the distinction of being the only youth band to rise to championship status.

224. The Real Cuckoo Company, with links to St. Mary's Church in Risca, performs musicals, pantomimes, variety shows, dances and festive celebrations. The intention of the Company was to enable youngsters to have fun, learn new talents and develop existing skills, all in a safe environment and under the umbrella of Christian fellowship. Since its establishment in 1994, the Company has performed an average of two shows a year.

The photograph shows local athletics hero, Jamie Baulch, paying a visit to the cast of the Real Cuckoo Company's production of Hood and his Merry Men of Sherwood, in 1998. The comedy was written by a member, Karen Johns.

225. A Musical Theme Park, the story of a family's day out to a theme park, was presented in 2001.

226. First Annual Concert of the then Risca Male Voice Choir, held at Trinity Church, Risca, in 1970.

227. Risca has had a long, albeit broken, history of male choirs dating back to the early 1900s. However the present illustrious choir had its genesis in 1970 when a group of seven like-minded souls with a love of singing gathered together in Risca Workingmen's Club with a view to forming a choir. From this uncertain and fledgling beginning, its membership rapidly increased. The first conductor, Les James, created a solid foundation and enabled the choir to develop a varied concert repertoire. The choir thrived but practices proved difficult because there were no permanent premises available. The choir was forced to move between clubs and pubs, leisure centres and schools. However in 1989 the choir was granted a lease on the old Risca Urban District Council Offices and over the years, thanks to much hard work by a band of dedicated choristers, the building was transformed into a wonderful and well-equipped head-quarters and rehearsal rooms.

Since its formation the choir has had just three musical directors - Les James (1970-1977), Alwyn Humphries (1977-1979), and Martin Hodson MBE (1979 to the present). Each of these talented musicians helped forge the choir's identity and enabled Risca to become one of the finest choirs in Wales. Martin Hodson in particular has used his great experience as a vocal coach, arranger and music interpreter to take the choir to an even higher level of musical sophistication.

Since 1973 the choir has performed an Annual Celebrity Concert and the first was held at Crosskeys College where the soloists were Cynthia Glover and Emlyn Ellis. The choir has also travelled extensively abroad to places like Germany, France, Belgium, the Czech Republic, Ireland, Spain, Gibraltar and also to California on three occasions. On one visit there they performed at the awe-inspiring Grace Cathedral in San Francisco. They have also performed in world famous venues closer to home such as The Millennium Centre, The Millennium Stadium and St. David's Hall in Cardiff.

Risca Choir has also enjoyed success in choral competitions including the title of Male Choir of the Year, winning the Welsh Choral Challenge Shield, The National Eisteddfod, The International Choral Festival of Jersey and the bronze medal at The International Choral Competition in Malta. The choir is also famous for its unique theme concerts at Christmas, one of which was turned into a feature length TV programme. Other TV appearances have included *The Magic of the Musicals* (which featured Bryn Terfel, Peter Karrie and Catherine Zeta Jones), The National Lottery First Birthday Broadcast and, in the summer of 1998, GMTV's Breakfast Show from St. Fagan's in Cardiff. The Choir continues to thrive even though the current membership stands at a lowly 54. It has an enviable reputation and continues to experiment and explore many musical styles and this diversity can be admired and enjoyed through its numerous recordings, the most successful of which is 2000's CD entitled *'We'll Keep A Welcome'* recorded with Bryn Terfel and the Orchestra of the Welsh National Opera which quickly reached gold status.

Gerald Pritchard/
Terry Richards/
Gorden Holly

228. A section of the Risca Male Choir at rehearsal in February 2007, under the musical direction of Martin Hodson, and with accompanist Julie Bevan

229. Oxford House Ladies Choir, c1967, with conductor Mrs Dorothy Davies-Jones, fifth from the left in the front row.

230. The Risca Support Group of St. David's Foundation at an Old Time Music Hall event at Crosskeys College in the early 1990s. Left to right:- Janet Price, ? Stephens, ? Eatwell, Madge Simms, Muriel Mould, Mary Tilley, Megan Loughman, Chris Browning and Norah Williams.

231. Cast of the play *'The Orchard Walls'* at St. Margaret's Church, Pontymister, June 1955. Left to right:- Joan Gillespie, John Allen, Freda Beddoe, Les Pritchard, Margaret Harrhy, Vi Pritchard, Peter Evans, Margaret Bowden, Graham Hayes, and Ruth Wallace.

Acknowledgements and Bibliography

The author's sincere thanks are due to the following who kindly allowed their photographs to be reproduced in this book:-
Abercarn Rugby Club (165, 166, 167); B. Baker (49, 71, 72, 92); R. Baulch (72, 73, 193, 194); Mrs. G. Beechey (28, 161, 198, 231); R. Beechey (187); Mrs. J. Britten (133); B. Coomer (143); Crosskeys Bowls Club (183, 184); Crosskeys Cricket Club (185, 186); www.crosskeys.me.uk (32, 71, 75); www.crumlinviaduct.co.uk. (41, 207); Crumlin Cricket Club (144, 145); Crumlin Rugby Club (146, 147, 148); J. Dance (142); R. Dowden (162, 163, 164); M. Gray (136,); Mrs. R. Gray (110, 112, 221, 223); J. Hatfield (62, 171, 172, 173, 174); N. Hicks (128, 129); Mrs. B Jones (106, 107, 134, 135, 175, 176, 204, 229); C. Jones (83); D. Jones (74); Mrs. P. Jones (113, 191); W. Jones (197); T. Jukes (76, 77); K. & P. Knight (18, 53, 54, 55, 56, 94, 95, 96, 98); Mrs. E. Leach (132); S. Lewis (65, 66, 67, 120, 222); Mrs. M. Loughman (24, 79, 81, 104, 105, 170, 179, 180, 219, 220); J. Maiden (99, 100, 101, 111, 116, 117); J. C. Maiden (89); P. Maiden (108); T. Maiden (216); D. Morgan (181, 182); www.newbridgeband.co.uk (205); J. Ollman (201, 202); D. Palmer (137); R. Pinney (208); Pontymister Welfare Bowls Club (199, 200); T. Powell (8, 209, 210); G. Pratt (123); Mrs. W. Prosser (24, 138); www.riscaunitedafc.co.uk (192); L. Rees (122); Risca Garages Ltd., (189, 190); Risca Male Choir (37, 226, 227); Risca Rugby Club (195, 196); S. Spooner (150); E. Southerley (47); N. Taylor (103); M. Thomas (48, 51, 68, 69); D. Tidmarsh (168, 169); J. Tidmarsh (177); Mrs. M. Treble (131); W. Watkins (4, 5, 6, 88, 90, 91, 151 152, 153, 203); Mrs. M. Warr (214, 215); Western Mail (159); Mrs. N. Williams (178, 230); Mrs. P. Williams (113, 118); T. Williams (206); Mrs. S. Wiltshire (224, 225); Ysgol Gymraeg Cwm Gwyddon (97).
The remainder of the photographs are from the author's own collection.

Other local publications:-
Glimpses of West Gwent, by Rex Pugh, 1934
Risca - Its Industrial and Social Development, by Alan Victor Jones, published by New Horizon, 1980.
Old Crumlin to Pontymister in Photographs, Volume 1, by Brian Collins and Terry Powell, published by Stewart Williams, Barry, 1981.
Old Blackwood and Lower Sirhowy Valley, by Brian Collins and Terry Powell, published by Stewart Williams, Barry, 1982.
Old Crumlin to Pontymister in Photographs, Volume 2, by Brian Collins and Terry Powell, published by Stewart Williams, Barry, 1982.
Man of the Valleys, edited by Mary Paget, Alan Sutton Publishing, 1985.
Old Abercarn Urban District including Pantside Newbridge and Crumlin, by David Taylor, published by Old Bakehouse Publications, Abertillery, 2000.
A Historical Tour around Mynyddislwyn Mountain, by Len Burland, published by Old Bakehouse Publications, Abertillery, 2002.
Crumlin to Pontymister, Then and Now, by Brian Collins and Terry Powell, published by Old Bakehouse Publications, Abertillery, 2003.
Coal, Guns and Rugby, by Alan Chivers, published by The Oakwood Press, 2005.
Crumlin to Pontymister, Places of Worship, by Brian Collins, published by Old Bakehouse Publications, Abertillery, 2005.

Some interesting local websites:-

www.crosskeys.me.uk
www.crumlinviaduct.co.uk
www.newbridgeband.co.uk
www.riscachoir.net

www.crosskeysband.co.uk
www.cwmcarnparagon.co.uk
www.newbridgememo.org.uk
www.riscamuseum.org.uk

Special thanks are due to my sister, Marjorie Maiden, for her valuable encouragement and support, Elizabeth Collins for her help in proof reading and to the management and staff of Old Bakehouse Publications for their friendship and help in the preparation of this work.